Reducing the Barriers to
International Trade
in Accounting Services

AEI STUDIES ON SERVICES TRADE NEGOTIATIONS
Claude E. Barfield, series editor

REDUCING THE BARRIERS TO INTERNATIONAL
TRADE IN ACCOUNTING SERVICES
Lawrence J. White

INSURANCE IN THE GENERAL AGREEMENT ON TRADE IN SERVICES
Harold D. Skipper, Jr.

Reducing the Barriers to International Trade in Accounting Services

Lawrence J. White

The AEI Press

Publisher for the American Enterprise Institute

WASHINGTON, D.C.
2001

Available in the United States from the AEI Press, c/o Publisher Resources Inc., 1224 Heil Quaker Blvd., P.O. Box 7001, La Vergne, TN 37086-7001. To order, call 1-800-937-5557. Distributed outside the United States by arrangement with Eurospan, 3 Henrietta Street, London WC2E 8LU, England.

ISBN 8447-7157-0

1 3 5 7 9 10 8 6 4 2

The AEI Press
Publisher for the American Enterprise Institute
1150 17th Street, N.W.
Washington, D.C. 20036

Printed in the United States of America

Contents

Foreword

The service sector accounts for more than 70 percent of the gross domestic product (GDP) of advanced industrial economies. Though trade in services is difficult to calculate and many transactions still go uncounted, current estimates place the worth of such trade as at least $2.5 trillion, or about a third of total world trade.

For the United States, the world's most advanced industrial economy, the service sector looms even larger. Services account for almost 80 percent of U.S. production and U.S. employment (while manufacturing accounts for 19 percent of U.S. GDP and 18 percent of U.S. employment). The surplus in U.S. services trade also partially offsets persistent U.S. merchandise trade deficits. In 1999, the services trade surplus was $76 billion; the merchandise deficit, $347 billion.

Despite the increasing importance of services trade and investment, only in 1995 did the multilateral trading system establish rules for opening markets in these economic sectors by negotiating the General Agreement on Trade in Services (GATS). This first effort at a discipline for services trade and investment created a framework of general principles and rules but left the large-scale liberalization of individual sectors to later negotiations.

Subsequently, under a mandate established as a part of the Uruguay Round negotiations, important advances toward real liberalization were achieved in two key sectors, telecommunications (1998) and financial services (1999), and services negotiations continued after the Round. In addition, members of the new World Trade Organization also committed themselves during the Uruguay Round to begin a new round of services trade negotiations in the year 2000.

Against this backdrop the American Enterprise Institute launched a new research project focusing on this next round of negotiations. Services 2000, as the new negotiations are called, are building on the unfinished agenda of the Uruguay Round and will, it is hoped, break new ground in areas such as market access liberalization, additional architectural reforms in the GATS structure, and horizontal (cross-sectoral) rulemaking regarding safeguards, government procurement, and subsidies.

The American Enterprise Institute project was mounted in conjunction with a group of other research institutions—the Kennedy School of Government at Harvard University and the Brookings Institution—and with the U.S. Coalition of Services Industries. AEI undertook a series of individual sectoral analyses. We commissioned papers on eight sectors: financial services (banks and securities), accounting, insurance, entertainment and culture, air freight and air cargo, airline passenger service, electronic commerce, and energy. Each study aimed to identify major barriers to trade liberalization in the sector under scrutiny and to present and assess liberalization policy options for trade negotiators and interested private-sector participants.

AEI would like to acknowledge the following donors for their generous support of the trade in services project, which provided some of the funding that allowed these studies to go forward: American Express Company, American International Group Inc., Enron Corporation, FedEx Corporation, Mastercard International Inc., the

Motion Picture Association of America, and the Mark Twain Institute. I emphasize, however, that the conclusions and recommendations of the individual studies are solely those of the authors.

Dissemination of the preliminary results of the research began even before the final drafts were finished. During 1999 and 2000, individual scholars made contributions to a series of meetings and conferences, including: the first World Services Congress in Atlanta and a preliminary agenda-setting seminar in Washington; and three international conferences in Chile, Costa Rica, and Hong Kong. In addition, AEI hosted conferences on financial services and transportation in Washington, and co-sponsored a conference on electronic commerce in Seattle. Further conferences are planned as the individual studies are published over the next year.

In this monograph, Lawrence J. White of the Stern School of Business at New York University analyzes the challenges facing GATS negotiators in the field of accounting and provides recommendations for meeting those challenges. Accounting services are part of a larger group of professional services that are of major importance for the United States, and a group of sectors in which America generally holds a strong comparative advantage. Analysts estimate that about 30 million Americans are employed in professional services such as accounting, law, architecture, and engineering. The combined sectors contribute about $10 billion to U.S. balance of payments receipts, according to figures compiled by the U.S. Department of Commerce.

Accounting is the most global of the professional services, and for that reason the World Trade Organization Working Party on Professional Services chose this sector as the first priority for achieving a detailed sectoral agreement under the new GATS. In addition, the Asian crisis in the late 1990s brought heightened urgency to the need for more sophisticated and analytically rigorous accounting rules. Policymakers and financial leaders widely agreed that poor accounting practices contributed to a lack of transparency regarding the true financial conditions of many manufacturing and financial institutions. In turn, inadequate investor information and a distrust of the integrity of available information impeded economic recovery in a number of Asian countries.

In this study White describes the "public good" aspect of the liberalization of accounting services by demonstrating that increased competition through market access leads to improved professional standards and ultimately to more efficient capital markets.

On the agenda of GATS 2000, two distinct sets of issues are the focus of negotiations: Market access and national treatment issues that fall under GATS Articles XVI and XVII, and domestic regulatory practices that fall under GATS Article VI.

Regarding market access issues, White lays out and rebuts much of the traditional rationale for excluding foreign competitors on the basis of consumer protection. He argues that the widespread market access "regulatory restrictions that [accounting] firms face force them into inefficient compromises that impede the flow of personnel and information and restrict organization forms and structures that would allow greater efficiency." And he identifies the major impediments that will form the basis for negotiations in the future and that will be overcome only by more liberal accounting sectoral commitments by individual WTO members.

Regarding differing domestic regulatory accounting frameworks, White analyzes the pros and cons of harmonization and mutual recognition. And he provides a list of pro-competitive regulatory principles that could accomplish the goal of establishing "best practices" that would serve as a model for gradual harmonization—and possibly the basis for an annex to the GATS accounting agreement (similar to the regulatory annex in the GATS telecommunications agreement).

Finally, this monograph and the accounting sector itself point up a continuing tension in service sector negotiations: domestic regulators can themselves become impediments to trade liberalization unless they are convinced that such liberalization serves the national interest. In the case of accounting services, the U.S. Securities and Exchange Commission has thus far opposed new international rules because of its belief that new World Trade Organization rules would dilute and weaken regulatory safeguards in this country. Thus, overcoming U.S. regulators' apprehensions presents as large a challenge for U.S. trade negotiators as overcoming opposition to accounting liberalization among other WTO member states.

CLAUDE E. BARFIELD
American Enterprise Institute

Acknowledgments

Thanks are due to Claude Barfield, Charles Heeter, John Hegarty, Harry Freeman, and Vincent Sacchetti for valuable comments on earlier drafts.

1
Introduction

Accountants and accounting are essential—though often undervalued—elements of the infrastructure of any enterprise. Information about a firm's financial accounts is vital for managers, owners, and creditors; it is a key input for lenders' and investors' decisions as to whether, when, and how to provide finance to enterprises.[1] Accounting is thus an important part of the business sector of any modern economy.

The growth of multinational enterprises generally, and of multinational accounting firms in particular, has focused attention on issues related to international trade in accounting services. This attention, in turn, is part of a rising tide of interest in trade in a wide range of services.

The street-level disruptions at the Seattle Ministerial Conference of the World Trade Organization in November and December 1999 were an unfortunate slowing of the general process of liberalizing international trade in goods and services. Given the momentum of more than five decades of international progress in reducing the barriers to trade in goods and the recent substantial interest in liberalizing trade in services, however, it seems likely that the Seattle events will represent only a brief stumble on the path to freer international trade.

Prior to the Ministerial Conference, substantial progress had been made with respect to establishing international commitments for freer trade in accounting services, and it seems likely that this progress will continue. The reasons for this progress, and why it matters, will be the major focus of this study.

2
Background

B eginning in the late 1970s, there was a growing realization that trade in services should be the next area to be targeted for reductions in trade barriers. Substantial progress had been made since the end of the Second World War in reducing barriers to trade in goods through a succession of multilateral negotiating "rounds" under the auspices of the General Agreement on Tariffs and Trade (GATT). Though international trade in goods was hardly free of all protectionist restraints, and considerably more progress could (and would) be made, trade in services had been largely untouched.

Trade in services became a major topic of discussion during the so-called Uruguay Round of GATT negotiations in the late 1980s. Those negotiations ultimately led to the creation of the World Trade Organization (WTO) as the successor to the GATT, and to a General Agreement on Trade in Services (GATS), which has served as the vehicle for the specific negotiations concerning reductions in the barriers to international trade in services.

A major initiative focusing on professional services has been included in these negotiations. The WTO Working Party on Professional Services (WPPS),[2] which came into existence in 1995, selected accounting as the first of the professional services areas for which a set of multilateral "disciplines" (rules that limit the protectionist nature of the domestic regulatory requirements that typically apply to accountants and accounting) would be developed. These multilateral disciplines were adopted by the WTO's Council on Trade in Services in December 1998 and will serve as the bases for reductions in international restrictions at the conclusion of future negotiations.[3] Prior to the adoption of the multilateral disciplines, the WPPS completed the development of guidelines for the negotiation of mutual recognition agreements (MRAs) that would apply to professional qualifications of accountants in various countries. These guidelines were adopted by the council in May 1997.

The choice of accounting as a lead sector for reducing barriers was not accidental. Accounting already has a substantial international component; the largest accounting firms have major international presences and have been eager to operate in less restrictive environments. Accounting is coming to be understood as a vital infrastructural element of financial services, and as finance becomes more global, accounting too should become more global. Similarly, as large business enterprises generally have increased their international operations, their need for international accounting services has grown.

Despite the considerable international presences of the major accounting firms, however, virtually all countries maintain various types of restrictions that impede the flow of accounting services across borders. The broad provisions of the GATS and the multilateral accounting disciplines that were adopted by the WTO in 1998 will apply only after further negotiations are completed. In the interim, WTO members are committed to a "standstill" arrangement: they will refrain from imposing heightened barriers to trade in accounting services.[4]

The substantial barriers that are currently in place provide prime targets for efforts to reduce and remove restrictions. Even in the wake of the Seattle experience, substantial progress can and should be made.

3

Why International Trade in Services Is (and Is Not) Different from Trade in Goods

In many respects international trade in services is importantly different from trade in goods. Indeed, the fact that multilateral negotiations on trade in services began in earnest *four decades* after the beginning of multilateral negotiations on trade in goods is a testament to this difference.

Nonetheless, there is at least one important way in which trade in services is not different: it provides the potential for improving a country's allocation of resources and thus raising its overall standard of living. This chapter will first explore the latter notion, in order to motivate the general discussion in this study of the importance of reducing the barriers to international trade in accounting services. We will then turn to the important ways that services are different.

Trade in Services Is Not Different: Improving Efficiency

The basic economics argument for reducing or eliminating impediments to trade rests on the improvements in efficiency in the allocation of a country's resources that result from such actions.[5] In essence, trade allows a country to focus its resources and energies on what it does relatively better than the rest of the world, importing those things that it does less well and paying for its imports by exporting the things that it does especially well. Though there are legitimate theoretical exceptions that can be offered to the free-trade argument, the fundamental case for free trade is a powerful one, and it has now been buttressed by decades of empirical evidence indicating that reduced barriers to trade generally have had the beneficial effects that have been promised.

Though the case for free trade is almost always couched in terms of flows of goods, the same principles are equally valid when applied to trade in services. If a country is relatively less efficient at producing a set of services than are some other countries, then the first country will generally be better off by allowing the others to supply those services and instead focusing its resources on the goods and services in which it is relatively more efficient.

At its heart, the case for the beneficial consequences of free (or freer) trade is just the case for competitive markets, expanded to an international context. The case for competitive markets is as applicable to services as it is to goods; so is the case for free trade.

The Ways in Which Trade in Services Is Different

Understanding international trade in goods is relatively straightforward: goods can be seen. They move physically across borders. Their movement is easy to visualize, as are many of the impediments to their movement: tariffs, quotas, and even more subtle impediments, such as customs delays at borders and regulatory procedures that favor national producers over foreign producers.

Trade in services is different, in at least two important ways. First, services are usually intangible. They cannot be seen, held, touched, or smelled. They usually do not physically cross borders the way that goods do. Second, services are often extensively regulated by governments—more often than is true for goods. Appreciating both differences is useful for understanding why liberalization negotiations have been slower for services than for goods.

Intangibility. Because services are invisible (indeed, international services remittances are sometimes described as part of "invisibles" in discussions of a country's balance of payments), they are not delivered in the same way as is true for goods. The following four methods of delivery are listed in Article I of the GATS and are frequently described as the four modes of supply under the GATS.

Cross-border. Some services do actually cross borders. This is true for electricity and electronic information and also for some financial services (for example, a bank that has its offices in country A may grant a loan to or accept a deposit from a customer that is located in country B). But these services do not stop and wait at a port of entry while a customs official inspects and categorizes them and levies a duty. Instead, they move instantaneously and invisibly.

Consumption abroad. Some services involve the travel of the customer from country B to the location of the enterprise that offers the services in country A. Tourism is a common example.

Commercial presence. Some services may best be delivered through the establishment of a physical presence at one or more specific locations. For example, a bank that is headquartered in country A may prefer to establish a branch location in country B in order to do business with customers in the latter country. Many long-term service relationships are best developed and enhanced through the local presence of physical establishments.

Temporary presence (presence of natural persons). Some services may be provided on a temporary basis, through the nationals of country A visiting country B to deliver the services. Entertainment services (such as concerts by visiting orchestras or rock stars), short-term consultancies, or construction services can be delivered in this fashion.

Some services can be delivered through a combination of two or more of these methods.

The commercial presence method is common in services, but this commercial presence means that the delivery of the service in country B will require a services firm that is headquartered in country A to make investments in country B in order to establish that location. In addition, personnel from the service deliverer's headquarters will have to visit the branch location in country B to deliver services, to hire local personnel, and to supervise those personnel. This need for investment and staffing that must originate from country A in order to deliver services in country B clearly makes the process of delivering services across borders more complicated than is true for the simple shipment of goods, and it provides greater and more subtle opportunities for governments to impede the flow of services. Restrictions on inbound foreign investment (including ownership structures and arrangements), on immigration, and on commercial location and establishment will all restrict the inflow of services.

The delivery of accounting services is highly dependent on the physical presence of local establishments (the commercial presence method). In addition, the larger accountancy firms (see chapter 4) make liberal use of short-term consultancies (the temporary presence method) in their efforts to mobilize specific sources of expertise within their firms. Whether the continuing technological revolution in telecommunications and data processing will allow accounting firms to be less dependent on these methods and instead to provide more of their services from afar—the cross-border method—remains an open question.

As will be discussed in chapter 5, given the current methods of delivering accounting services, the types of restrictions discussed above are indeed important impediments to the flow of accounting services.

Regulation. Services are more susceptible to various forms of governmental regulation or outright government ownership. As of the 1970s, the typical list of industries in the United States that were described as "heavily regulated" (or, outside of the United States, were either regulated or in the hands of governments) included transportation services (air, rail, road, water), telecommunications services (broadcasting, telephony), financial services (banking, insurance, securities), and electricity.[6] These industries became the prime targets for the deregulation efforts of the late 1970s and the 1980s in the United States (and for deregulation and privatization efforts in other countries). Despite the substantial deregulation that has occurred, however, these sectors continue to be more regulated than most other areas of the U.S. economy.[7]

In addition, professional services (for example, medicine, law, accounting, architecture, and engineering) have been subject to extensive direct and indirect governmental regulation. The direct form of regulation occurs through the actions of formal government agencies. The indirect form occurs when governments delegate to professional organizations many of the regulatory roles that would otherwise be exercised by government; even when such roles are delegated, the ultimate regulatory powers are still held by governments.

The reasons for the extensive government involvement in the delivery of these services vary, but consumer protection is a common theme.[8] In turn, consumer protection may be couched either in terms of protection against the exercise of monopoly power or in terms of protection against the abuses that could arise from the complicated nature of the services and the superior knowledge of the services provider vis-à-vis the customer.[9] But it is an easy jump from regulation that is supposed to protect consumers to regulation that is "captured" by the regulated entities; in the latter case, regulation may well harm consumers by protecting the incumbent services providers from the rigors of competition.[10]

The extensive overlay of regulation of many services thus adds important elements to any efforts to liberalize international trade in these services. First, the regulation is present, and arguably it is there for a reason. Efforts to liberalize trade have to confront the question of whether trade in services is compatible with the protections that the regulation is supposed to provide. Next, extra procedures, extra laws, and extra agencies must be dealt with. Finally, the incumbent firms can wrap themselves in the mantle of consumer protection and argue to home-country government officials that this protection will be weakened if providers from abroad are allowed under the tent. As will be discussed in chapter 5, these patterns of professional-services regulation apply squarely to accounting.

In sum, services are different from goods. Their mode of delivery and their tendency to be regulated have created delays and extra barriers to the opening of trade in services. Indeed, the structure of the GATS recognizes these differences and sets less ambitious goals for the dismantling of barriers in the services areas than is true for goods. Nevertheless, the GATS represents a substantial effort toward freer trade in services, and accounting services are an important part of that effort. We now turn to a deeper exploration of accounting services.

4

Accounting Services in International Trade

The scope of "accounting services" [11] is usually understood to include accounting and bookkeeping (measuring and recording the financial flows and positions of an enterprise), auditing (verifying and attesting/certifying the accuracy of the financial position and results of the enterprise, for internal or external purposes), and tax preparation. Clearly, the three activities are closely related.

In addition, over the past few decades the largest accounting firms—especially in the United States—have become actively involved in management consulting, and growth in this area has been considerably more rapid than for the firms' more traditional services. As can be seen in table 1, as of 1998 management consulting contributed almost half (47 percent) of the domestic revenues of the hundred largest U.S. accounting firms, with accounting, auditing, and tax services contributing the remainder (53 percent). For the largest of the large—the "Big Five"[12] firms—the corresponding percentages were 51 percent and 49 percent, respectively. For the Big Five, their defining services are no longer their dominant sources of revenues![13] Between 1997 and 1998 management consulting revenues grew by 38 percent for both the largest hundred and the Big Five.

Table 1: Percentages of Domestic Revenues Attributable to Major Lines of Activity, Largest U.S. Accounting Firms, 1998

	Largest Hundred Firms	Largest Five Firms
Accounting/Auditing	30%	30%
Tax	23	19
Management consulting	47	51
Total	100%	100%

Source: *Accounting Today,* "The Top 100 Firms," Special Supplement (March 15–April 4, 1999), p. 5.

Management consulting has been a natural, synergistically related service for the large accounting firms. Through the provision of their traditional accounting, auditing, and tax services, they acquire a considerable amount of detailed information about an enterprise's operations, to which they then apply additional expertise to help the enterprise develop and achieve its tactical and strategic goals. One of the latest facets of management consulting by accounting firms—information systems consulting—is again a synergistic use of their expertise as information handlers and users.

The auditing function of these firms has gained special significance in the past few decades as publicly traded companies and the securities markets have risen in importance. Investors in and lenders to publicly traded enterprises rely heavily on an enterprise's audited financial statements as an accurate statement of its financial position and results. Bond covenants and banks' lending agreements often contain restrictions couched in terms of the financial flows and positions of the borrowing enterprise, measured according to generally accepted accounting principles (GAAP) and certified through an audited financial statement. Indeed, the certification value of the Big Five accounting firms has become so great that virtually all of the "Fortune 500" U.S.-based companies are audited by the Big Five, and a high fraction of the next five hundred are also audited by the Big Five. If the largest three[14] of the next tier of accounting firms are included, the coverage of the "Fortune 1,000" is virtually complete.[15] Similarly, when young companies first issue securities through initial public offerings (IPOs), the investment bankers and underwriters that shepherd the new issues into the securities markets almost always insist on the certifying value of one of these eight largest accounting firms.

As another indication of the dominance of the Big Five firms, in 1999 the hundred largest accounting firms in the United States had aggregate revenues of about $31 billion (including management consulting revenues); the Big Five constituted 89.9 percent of this total.[16]

The International Dimension

Despite the limitations and restrictions on their international activities that will be discussed in the next chapter, the largest accounting firms have all developed substantial international presences. Much of this expansion has occurred as a consequence of the international growth of their clients and the desire of the individual clients to retain their accounting firms across international boundaries. The expertise and prestige of the largest accounting firms have also allowed them to acquire overseas clients that have no roots in the accounting firms' home countries and to affiliate with local accounting firms, forming networks and partnerships under a common brand name.

The overall effects have been striking. Though four of the Big Five accounting firms are headquartered in the United States (the fifth, KPMG, is headquartered in Amsterdam but has a strong U.S. presence and orientation), the Big Five now derive approximately 65 percent of their revenues from locations outside of the United States.[17] Table 2 lists the

twenty largest accounting firms or networks and the number of countries in which each firm operates. The Big Five
tend to be in the most locations, but even the smaller firms
can be found in dozens of countries.

**Table 2: The Twenty Largest International Accounting
Firms/Networks and the Number of Countries in Which Each Has
Operations,1998–99**

PricewaterhouseCoopers	150
Andersen Worldwide	81
Ernst & Young International	133
KPMG International	157
Deloitte Touche Tohmatsu	135
BDO International	86
Grant Thornton International	91
Horwath International	86
RSM International[a]	74
Moores Rowland International	87
Summit International Associates	58
Nexia International	78
PKF International	108
Fiducial International	60
HLB International	90
Moore Stephens International	75
AGN International	67
MacIntyre Strater International	83
IGAF	57
BKR International	60

[a] Includes McGladrey & Pullen.
Sources: *Accountancy International* 124 (August 1999): 8; WTO
(1998, p. 4).

The Big Five are also by far the largest accounting firms in
the world, as is indicated in table 3. As can be seen, the Big
Five together account for 77 percent of the revenues of the
forty largest international accounting networks, and there is
a sharp drop between the sizes of the fifth firm (Deloitte)
and the sixth (BDO). Further, of the hundred largest firms
worldwide (as measured by market value at the end of
1999), the Big Five audited ninety-eight of them.[18]

Table 3: Sizes of the Forty Largest International Accounting Firms/Networks, 1998–99

	Revenue ($ billions)	No. of Offices	No. of Partners	No. of Prof. Staff
PricewaterhouseCoopers	15.3	1,183	10,000	146,000
Andersen Worldwide	13.9	412	2,788	93,916
Ernst & Young	10.9	675	6,200	58,700
KPMG	10.4	825	6,790	64,510
Deloitte Touche Tohmatsu	9.0	725	5,608	60,790
Total for Big Five:	59.5	3,820	31,386	292,516
BDO International	1.6	510	1,732	12,176
Grant Thornton International	1.5	584	2,335	12,725
Horwath International	1.2	369	1,790	11,280
RSM International[a]	1.2	524	1,864	10,623
Moores Rowland International	1.1	603	1,884	10,717
Total for next five:	6.6	2,590	9,605	57,521
Total for next thirty:	11.2	6,964	19,169	114,924
Grand total for all forty:	77.3	13,374	60,160	464,961
Big Five as a percentage of grand total:	77%	29%	52%	63%

[a] Includes McGladrey & Pullen.
Source: *Accountancy International* 124 (August 1999): 8.

It is also worth noting that, of the dozen largest account-ing firms worldwide, nine are headquartered in the United States, two are headquartered in the United Kingdom, and one is headquartered in the Netherlands. These firms thus have a strong North American and west European orienta-tion. The global dominance of transatlantic-oriented firms is partly explained by the worldwide presence of large North American and west European corporations generally (and the desire of these corporations to retain their domestic accounting firms as they expand abroad) and partly by the large base that these transatlantic economies have provided and the greater relative importance of accounting and auditing in the economies, securities markets, and securities laws of these countries (especially the United States and the United Kingdom).

As tables 2 and 3 indicate, the international accounting firms are often described as "networks." The firms themselves are always partnerships, and their affiliations and alliances across international borders are fluid and varied; indeed, in the international context, the characterization of the large firms as "partnerships of partnerships" is quite apt.[19] The annual data compilation in *Accountancy International,* from which the data for tables 2 and 3 were drawn, has a separate column for the number of "member firms" that comprise each of the major networks. Ernst & Young, for example, lists 123 member firms; KPMG lists 146.

These fluid and varying arrangements with respect to local affiliates are often adaptations and accommodations to the local limitations imposed by national governments (to be discussed in the next chapter). Nevertheless, despite these limitations, the brand name of each of the large firms—especially the Big Five—is important.

The international presence and dominance by the large U.S.-headquartered (or U.S.-oriented) accounting firms affect the U.S. balance of payments. In 1998 U.S. direct exports of "accounting, auditing, and bookkeeping services" plus "management, consulting, and public relations services" totaled $2 billion, while imports of the same categories of services totaled $1.2 billion, yielding a net export surplus of $0.8 billion.[20] In 1996 the sales of "accounting, research, management, and related services" by overseas affiliates of U.S. firms to foreign purchasers totaled $7.7 billion, while the U.S. affiliates of foreign companies sold $2 billion of the same category of services to U.S. purchasers;[21] the net exports by U.S. firms thus amounted to $5.7 billion.

Despite the substantial international presences of the large accounting firms and the magnitude of their transactions, the extensive local regulation of accounting services makes the firms' international operations more difficult and costly than would otherwise be the case. It is to these impediments that we now turn.

5

The Impediments to Trade
in Accounting Services

As a professional service (like medicine, law, architecture, or engineering), accounting has been subject to substantial domestic regulation in virtually all countries.[22] Though the detailed requirements vary from country to country, accountants typically must satisfy education and practical experience requirements and a local residency requirement; in some countries, they must also pass a qualifying or licensing exam. The organizational structure of accounting firms is typically restricted as well. Accounting firms are often limited to partnerships or sole proprietorships; corporate forms are often prohibited; and ownership of accounting firms is often limited to accounting professionals.

Further, the forms and procedures involved in the service itself—for example, accounting standards and auditing procedures—are usually regulated. Sometimes, restrictions or bans are placed on advertising or on other forms of promotion and price competition.

Regulation usually occurs at the national level, but in some countries—notably, the United States, Canada, and Australia—regulation has devolved to the state or province level and varies among jurisdictions.[23] Regulation may be carried out by formal governmental agencies or delegated to professional organizations (or combined in a mixture of the two).

The primary goal of such restrictions is consumer protection: to ensure that only qualified individuals provide the service; that the integrity, quality, independence, and objectivity of the service and the service provider are maintained; that conflicts of interest are minimized; and that aggrieved consumers have an opportunity to obtain redress.

The goal of consumer protection can be readily subverted, however. The restrictions constitute barriers to entry: if enforced perfectly, they would exclude only the charlatans and quacks, but incumbent providers will always realize that the restrictions—perhaps, with some supplements—can also be used to exclude competitors more broadly. Further, as technologies change and improve, and as customer competence and capabilities develop, regulatory restrictions that might have been necessary (or at worst harmless) in one era may later become inappropriate and seriously distortional. But the forces of inertia, buttressed by the vested interests of protected incumbents, are more powerful when regulatory institutions and procedures are in place.

This appears to be the case for accounting services. As was documented in chapter 4, the major accounting firms are international in structure; international trade in accounting (and related) services is a substantial reality. But the widespread local regulatory restrictions that these firms face force them into inefficient compromises that impede the flow of personnel and information and restrict organizational forms and structures that would allow greater efficiency. The inevitable consequence is higher costs, poorer service to clients, and reduced efficiency.

The following are examples of restrictions and restraints imposed by one or more countries that favor domestic incumbents and discriminate against noncitizen providers, thereby inhibiting trade and efficiency in accounting services:[24]

- nationality requirements with respect to who can offer local accounting services
- residence or establishment requirements
- restrictions on the international mobility of accounting personnel
- restrictions as to the use of the brand names of firms, or requirements that only local names be used
- restrictions on advertising or other promotional efforts
- restrictions on price competition
- quantitative limits on the provision of services
- restrictions on the services that accounting firms can and cannot provide
- restrictions on who can be an owner of an accounting firm; for example, requirements that all (or a specified number or fraction) of the owners of an accounting firm be local citizens, be residents, be active in the business of the firm, be locally licensed, or be members of an approved professional organization
- restrictions as to the legal form or structure that an accounting firm must have (for example, prohibitions on a corporate form)
- discriminatory arrangements with respect to the licensing of foreign accountants, including applications, testing, and assessments of educational qualifications and relevant experience
- differential taxation treatment
- restrictions on international payments for services
- restrictions on cross-border flows of information
- inadequate protections for the intellectual property related to accounting services, such as computer software
- "buy national" practices of governments with respect to their purchases of accounting services

It is worth noting that even in instances in which the restrictions appear to affect domestic incumbents and foreign entrants similarly (for example, restrictions on advertising), the effect is likely to be differentially adverse to the foreign entrant, since the entrant may need advertising or other promotion to enter and expand in a market dominated by domestic incumbents.

In many instances the larger accounting networks are prevented from expanding and strengthening their international presences. Since the cultures of these larger networks are those of relatively high accounting and auditing standards, an ironic consequence of these restrictions (for a professional service in which a major rationale for local regulation is consumer protection and the maintenance of high quality) is that quality standards for accounting and auditing in many countries are lower than they otherwise could be.

Compilations similar to the list above have been available since at least the early 1980s.[25] As the interest in trade in services has grown and as negotiations have become more substantive in the 1990s, the compilations have become more frequent as well.[26] Comparisons of the lists from the 1980s with those of the 1990s show a striking similarity in the types and nature of the restrictions.

Though simple comparisons cannot by themselves indicate the presence or absence of any progress in the removal of restrictions, there is a strong sense that progress has been only modest. Indeed, the absence of immediate progress in reducing barriers contributed to the International Federation of Accountants' disappointment with the WTO's adoption of the multilateral disciplines at the end of 1998. There is thus considerable room for future negotiations to convert into reality many countries' expressions of their intent to remove restrictions.

6

Differing Accounting Standards: How Important Is Harmonization?

The differing accounting frameworks or standards that are in use in different countries are often described as one of the barriers to trade in accounting services. They are at most a modest barrier: their importance is greater in the operations of international capital markets (and in the operations of international enterprises more generally) than in accounting services.

Nevertheless, because the issues of differing accounting standards and potential harmonization of standards are frequently linked to discussions of liberalization of international trade in accounting services,[27] and because they are important in their own right, they deserve some discussion here.[28]

Are Differing Accounting Standards a Barrier to Liberalization?

In principle, the differing accounting frameworks that are in force in different countries are a barrier to the liberalization of trade in accounting services. They place extra burdens on international firms and make the movement of personnel somewhat more costly; incumbent domestic firms thereby gain a modest advantage vis-à-vis foreign firms. The problem of differing standards appears on many lists of impediments to freer trade.

But differing accounting frameworks have not been adopted or manipulated as a specific effort to protect domestic accountants against entrants from abroad. Further, the international accounting firms face similar burdens with respect to differing local languages and legal systems. The international accounting firms readily adapt to those challenges, and they have readily adapted to differing accounting standards. Differing accounting frameworks appear to be a modest barrier at most. If harmonization proves to be worthwhile, it will be for the reasons discussed below and not as a major initiative to liberalize trade in accounting services.

The Value of Accounting Harmonization— and Some Cautions

The real value of harmonizing on a common accounting system lies elsewhere—in reducing international enterprises' accounting costs, in helping to integrate international capital markets, and in serving as the guise whereby countries with deficient accounting frameworks are induced to improve their accounting standards. But harmonization also has drawbacks that warrant discussion.

Reducing accounting costs. To the extent that an enterprise operates in different jurisdictions and must prepare financial reports for the different jurisdictions according to differing accounting frameworks, its costs are higher than they would be if a single framework were used. Further, to the extent that the enterprise additionally uses another framework for its own informational purposes, its costs are yet higher.

Integrating international capital markets. As the rapid technological improvements in telecommunications and data processing dramatically reduce the costs of transmitting and analyzing information, providers and users of capital around the globe are increasingly being brought into trans- actions with each other. To the extent that the borrowers and users employ differing accounting frameworks among them- selves, the tasks of the lenders and investors in comparing and assessing risks and prospects are made more difficult; in the parlance of microeconomics, differing accounting frame- works increase the transaction costs of operating in interna- tional capital markets. Harmonization to a common standard can reduce those transaction costs and can pro- mote the smoother flow of capital across international boundaries.[29]

Improving deficient standards. Where countries have defi- cient accounting frameworks—as is often the case in devel- oping countries—an effort at international harmonization (which takes the developed world's standards as its general base) could serve as the means for raising the quality of the accounting frameworks in those countries. Arguably, a sim- ilar process has been at work with respect to the interna- tional harmonization of capital requirements for banks.[30]

Some cautions. The case for harmonization to reduce the costs of capital is strongest where the accounting differences are arbitrary and serve no useful distinguishing purposes or where harmonization is the guise for strengthening (for example, increasing the transparency of) a country's weak accounting framework. But the differences may reflect adap- tations to different characteristics of different economies, such as when an economy has had periodic bouts of severe inflation (which might call for revaluations of financial stocks and flows) or has experienced only modest inflation (which might call for the avoidance of the vagaries that could accompany revaluations).[31] Further, there are serious conceptual and philosophical questions as to whether financial accounting should have a stewardship focus, which would call for an orientation toward historical costs, or a current-value focus.

Accordingly, harmonization is not a win-only proposition. Valuable adaptations to local conditions may be lost, and serious alternatives may be discarded. Further, with a single harmonized standard, the opportunities for localized experimentation and development of new alternatives are eliminated. Rigidities in accounting may be exacerbated.

In sum, harmonization carries potential costs as well as benefits. A weighing of both is warranted before judgments are made.

Historical Developments

The International Accounting Standards Committee (IASC), created in 1973, is the main body that has focused on developing "international accounting standards" (IASs) that would be adopted internationally and thus would become the harmonized standard. The creation of the International Organization of Securities Commissions (IOSCO) in 1986, and its interest in the development of IASs, reinforced the mission of the IASC.

In 1995 the IOSCO and the IASC agreed that the latter should make a concerted effort to develop a set of core standards that the IOSCO could endorse and that its member countries could adopt for cross-border securities offerings and other foreign listings. In addition, the European Union (EU) encouraged its member states to allow their companies to use IASs and to accept the financial statements of companies from other member states (on a mutual recognition basis) for listing on each other's securities exchanges.

The IASC completed its tasks at the end of 1998, and decisions by the IOSCO and its constituent members are forthcoming.[32] The U.S. Securities and Exchange Commission (SEC) will play a crucial role. The SEC has historically resisted other countries' accounting standards, insisting that any non-U.S. company that wanted to have its securities publicly traded in the United States must restate its financial accounts to U.S. generally accepted accounting principles.[33] The U.S. Financial Accounting Standards Board (FASB) issued a lengthy report in late 1999[34] that was quite critical of the IASC's proposed standards.

Despite vaguely encouraging statements by SEC officials,[35] the basic message of the SEC in the past (and of the recent FASB report) is that other countries' standards, including the IASC's proposed standards, are not rigorous enough to protect investors in the U.S. securities markets. Consequently, it seems quite likely that the SEC will eventually reject the IASC's efforts as unnecessarily weakening the investor protections that are currently embodied in U.S. GAAP.

The consequences of such a decision would likely be less substantial than the partisans in the debate over IASs have indicated. Officials of the New York Stock Exchange, and others, have advocated adopting the IASC standards, or something similar, so as to enhance the role of the U.S. exchanges in international securities markets. They see the SEC requirement of restatement to U.S. GAAP as substantially raising the costs of a U.S. securities listing for non-U.S. companies and thereby discouraging U.S. listings and the use of the U.S. securities exchanges. What seems to be forgotten in this discussion is that a U.S. listing also carries with it obligations to abide by the entire panoply of federal securities laws, which are also seen as burdensome by non-U.S. companies. The elimination or modification of the U.S. GAAP requirement would not alter these other obligations and would thus likely lead to far fewer new listings than the advocates expect.

7

The Current Framework for Negotiations

Despite the Seattle experience, the WTO will likely remain an important forum for continued negotiations with respect to international trade in services. Negotiations on trade in accounting services should proceed ahead of many others because of the advances that have already been made, such as the multilateral disciplines and the guidelines on mutual recognition agreements. It is worth reviewing the structure of the GATS and its amplifications,[36] which will be the structure under which the negotiations will occur.[37]

The Structure of the GATS

The GATS, which came into effect on January 1, 1995, is an extensive document that applies to all WTO members (as of April 2000, there were 136 member countries) and is intended to cover a broad range of services and circumstances. The document contains general obligations of member countries and narrower obligations that apply only to member countries that commit or bind themselves to liberalized trade in specific services sectors.

With respect to accounting services, the most important general-obligation provisions of the GATS are as follows:[38]

- Article II establishes a general obligation for most-favored-nation (MFN) treatment.[39]
- Article III establishes a general obligation for transparency with respect to laws, regulations, administrative guidelines, and similar measures that are relevant to trade in services. The transparency should include opportunities for inquiry and notification of significant changes.
- Article VI applies to domestic regulation and requires members to ensure that qualification requirements and procedures, technical standards, and licensing requirements do not constitute unnecessary barriers to trade. Domestic regulatory requirements should be based on objective and transparent criteria, such as competence and the ability to supply the service; should not be more burdensome than necessary to ensure the quality of the service; and, with respect to licensing procedures, should not in themselves be a restriction on the supply of the service. Members must provide an objective and impartial means of reviewing and providing appropriate remedies for administrative decisions that affect trade in services.
- Article VII encourages mutual recognition of the qualifications of services providers. Member recognition of foreign qualifications should not constitute a means of discrimination among countries in standards or criteria. Multilateral processes are encouraged.

In addition to the general obligations, the most important specific obligations that apply when a country has made commitments with respect to a particular services sector (such as accounting) are as follows:[40]

- Article VI requires that measures of general application that affect trade in services be administered in a reasonable, objective, and impartial fashion. In addition, members should provide adequate procedures for the mutual recognition of the competence of other members.

- Article XVI applies to market access and prohibits specific limitations (such as quotas) on the number of suppliers, on the total value of service transactions or assets (including needs tests), on the total number of service operations or total quantity of service output, on the total number of people that may be employed, on the types of legal entity or joint venture through which a service can be supplied, and on the participation of foreign capital.

- Article XVII requires "national treatment"; that is, members should accord to foreign services and service suppliers treatment that is no less favorable than is applied to domestic services and suppliers. Specific treatment can be different, so long as the resultant conditions of competition do not favor domestic services or service suppliers.

Additional Measures

Both the general and the for-the-committed-only GATS obligations are broadly worded. Detailed negotiations are required to flesh out these broad provisions. In order to facilitate these negotiations as applied to the accountancy sector, the WTO's Council for Trade in Services has adopted two additional measures that were developed by its Working Party on Professional Services. First, in May 1997, the council adopted nonbinding guidelines for mutual recognition agreements (MRAs) for the accountancy sector, which amplify the provisions of Article VII of the GATS. The guidelines provide an extensive framework that is intended to help members structure their MRAs in ways that make them transparent and accessible.

Second, in December 1998 the council adopted disciplines (rules) on domestic regulation of the accountancy sector that amplify the provisions of Article VI.[41] The disciplines provide greater detail as to transparency, licensing requirements and procedures, qualification requirements and procedures, and technical standards.

The disciplines implicitly recognize that regulation of accountancy is ubiquitous, but they require members to ensure that such regulation is not more trade-restrictive than is necessary to fulfill legitimate objectives, which include protecting consumers and ensuring quality of service, professional competency, and the integrity of the profession. With respect to licensing, the disciplines urge alternatives to residency requirements (for example, allowing the posting of security bonds to serve as an alternative method of ensuring accountability); acknowledge professional organization membership requirements but require reasonable terms of membership; require that the use of firm names not be restricted (except in fulfillment of a legitimate objective—such as preventing consumer confusion); and require that licensing procedures be transparent and not unnecessarily burdensome.

With respect to qualifications, the disciplines require transparency and reasonable procedures regarding examinations and other qualifications; they also require a link between the qualifications and the activities for which the authorization is sought. Members are required to take account of qualifications (such as education, experience, and examinations) that have been acquired in other countries. They are encouraged to note the role that MRAs can play in facilitating the verification of qualifications or establishing their equivalency.

With respect to technical standards (that is, accounting standards or frameworks themselves), the disciplines require that such standards be prepared, adopted, and applied only to fulfill legitimate objectives.[42]

Finally, the disciplines will not come into force until the *conclusion* of the round of services negotiations that was started in 2000; until that time, the members cannot raise new barriers to trade in accountancy services.

An Evaluation

It is tempting, and easy, to be pessimistic about the prospects for trade liberalization in services. In important respects, the GATS and its amplifications represent a somewhat tentative approach to liberalized trade. It is riddled with exemptions: member countries can simply decide on the sectors for which they wish to commit to the obligations of Article XVI (market access), Article XVII (national treatment), and parts of Article VI (domestic regulation); even for committed sectors, members can still list and maintain restrictions; and even a general obligation like MFN (Article II) can be avoided for specific sectors. Further, the accountancy disciplines did not tackle market access and national treatment issues, such as residency and citizenship requirements and more rigorous requirements for foreign applicants than for domestic applicants.

In addition, despite the fact that they went into effect in 1995, the general principles of the GATS (and the more specific details of the accountancy disciplines of 1998) will not have a positive impact in reducing barriers to trade in services (though they will prevent the raising of new barriers) until the conclusion of negotiations that began in 2000. Given the experiences of past rounds of trade negotiations (and the experience of the 1999 Seattle disruptions), this conclusion might not occur until the middle of the decade. Thus, the real impact of the GATS might be delayed for almost a decade.

Despite this multitude of limitations, pessimism with respect to the future of trade liberalization in services is not warranted.[43] The GATS is a new phenomenon with respect to multilateral agreements for services, and, as was discussed in chapters 3 and 5 of this study, services are a highly sensitive area in which domestic regulation is widespread and in which domestic sovereignty issues remain potent. As the fifty years of experience with the GATT have indicated, completely free trade is an unrealistic goal, even over a five-decade period. Progress is slow; the forces of protectionism are powerful. But the extent of progress in the GATT has been substantial, and the trend remains positive.

The same realistic perspective should be applied to any appraisal of the GATS. Progress will be slow, especially since services are a more sensitive area. The GATS does represent progress; the political imperative will be to keep the momentum going in the direction of freer trade.

8

The Road Ahead

As of early 1999 there had been commitments by sixty-seven members[44] of the WTO (of which twenty-six were developed countries[45] and forty-one represented developing and transition economies[46]) with respect to accounting, auditing, and bookkeeping services. Though these sixty-seven countries represent only half of the WTO's membership, they represent about 90 percent of international revenues for accounting services.[47] Detailed analyses of these commitments, however, indicate that many fall far short of a total embrace of free trade in accounting services.[48] Also, as would be expected, the commitments by the developing and transition economies' governments are more limited than those of the developed-country governments.[49] And the extent of restrictions in commitments is greater for the commercial presence and temporary presence modes of delivery, which are the important modes for accounting, than for the remaining two modes. Still, the commitments represent a starting point for negotiations and provide opportunities for further openings.

The basic principles encouraged by the GATS—MFN treatment (Article II), transparency (Article III), restraining domestic regulation to legitimate ends (Article VI), mutual recognition (Article VII), market access (Article XVI), and national treatment (Article XVII)—should be vigorously pursued. Along these lines, the first goal should be the elimination of the most egregious forms of regulatory protection of domestic accounting entities. Such regulations clearly have little to do with consumer protection and are fundamentally anticonsumer, because they raise costs or reduce the quality of accounting services. The forms of regulation that should be eliminated (along with the GATS provisions that are likely to apply) include the following:

- restrictions on the use of foreign firms' brand names (Article VI and disciplines)
- restrictions on the mobility of personnel (Article XVI)
- discriminatory taxation (Article XVII)
- discriminatory licensing arrangements (Article VI and disciplines; Article XVI)
- quantitative limits on the provision of services (Article VI and disciplines; Article XVI)
- restrictions on legal structural forms (Article XVI)
- restrictions on advertising, promotion, and pricing (Article VI; Article XVI)
- "buy national" policies (Article XIII; Article XVI; Article XVII)
- nationality, residence, or establishment requirements (Article VI and disciplines; Article XVI; Article XVII)
- ownership restrictions (Article VI; Article XVI; Article XVII)

This is an ambitious agenda. Wherever possible, negotiators should focus on the general obligation articles (Articles II and III and parts of Article VI) rather than the for-the-committed only articles (Articles XVI and XVII).

If all or most of these restrictions can be eliminated among most of the WTO's 136 members, much will be achieved. Attention can then be turned to the tougher questions of mutual recognition of qualifications (Article VII),[50] protection of intellectual property, and restrictions on payments (Article XII).

These negotiations are not likely to be easy. The heavy hands of domestic regulation will surely be important inertial forces. But the Asian financial crises of 1997 should provide added power and urgency to the arguments favoring freer trade in accounting services, especially in developing and transition economies. It is clear that poor accounting practices by local banks and other important local enterprises in a number of Asian countries were partially responsible for the problems that arose. Liberalized trade in accounting services would provide greater opportunities for entry and for greater local influence by the large international accounting firms. In turn, these large firms—with their greater ability to mobilize expertise, their general culture of higher accounting standards, and their substantial international reputations at stake—are likely to be strong forces for more reliable accounting and auditing.[51] Indeed, the World Bank apparently has informally asked the Big Five to avoid signing financial statements that, although prepared in accordance with local accounting standards, are below prevailing international standards.[52] In an era of the increasing globalization of financial markets, this strengthening of the accounting and auditing function in many countries should help increase their access to those markets.[53]

9

Conclusion

Accounting is an essential infrastructural element of the business sector in any modern economy; it is crucial for finance. Efficiency in the way that accounting services are delivered can enhance the efficiency of the rest of the economy.

The large accounting firms are already international in scope and operation, but national regulatory restrictions diminish their ability to operate fluidly across national boundaries in ways that would best serve their clients. International trade in accounting services is substantially impaired.

The GATS negotiations that began in 2000 hold promise for important liberalizations of trade in accounting services. These negotiations should be pursued vigorously, with efforts to increase the number of countries involved, to expand their commitments, and to conclude the negotiations promptly. The gains from this vigorous pursuit will be substantial.

Notes

1. For discussions of the role of information, including accounting information, in the processes of finance, see White (1998) and Goldberg and White (2001).
2. The WPPS has since been transformed into the Working Party on Domestic Regulation.
3. For a general discussion of the adoption of these disciplines, see Ascher (1999).
4. It was the absence of immediate progress, as well as concerns about the weakness of the disciplines, that caused the International Federation of Accountants (IFAC) to express tepid support for the disciplines; see IFAC (1998).
5. The case for free trade can be found in any international economics text; see, for example, Yarbrough and Yarbrough (1997).
6. The natural gas industry was also heavily regulated in the United States, and the price regulation of petroleum that began during the general wage and price controls of the early 1970s persisted through the late 1970s.
7. For example, the U.S. airline industry was substantially deregulated between 1978 and 1984. Nevertheless, there remains today a ceiling of 25 percent foreign ownership that applies to any airline that serves domestic routes. Effectively, foreign ownership of domestic U.S. airlines is not permitted. Similar restrictions apply to ocean shipping; see White (1988) and Fox and White (1997).
8. See, for example, Mills and Young (1999).
9. In more formal economics terms, this latter problem is frequently described as the problem of asymmetric information.
10. See, for example, Stigler (1971), Posner (1974), and Peltzman (1976).
11. See, generally, Weinstein (1987) and Most (1993).
12. These firms are PricewaterhouseCoopers, Arthur Andersen, Ernst & Young, KPMG Peat Marwick, and Deloitte & Touche.
13. By contrast, in the mid-1980s, accounting and auditing were responsible for well over half of the revenues of the large account-

ing firms, and tax services and management consulting were each responsible for well under a third; see Rossi (1986).

14. Grant Thornton, BDO Seidman, and McGladrey & Pullen.

15. A study of the auditors of the largest publicly traded nonfinancial companies, as of 1995, found that the Big Six (now Big Five) audited all 241 of the companies with assets over $5 billion, 548 of the 551 companies with assets between $1 billion and $5 billion, and 363 of the 372 companies with assets between $0.5 billion and $1 billion; see Doogar and Easley (1998).

16. See *Accountancy International,* Vol. 124, October 1999, p. 8.

17. This estimate is derived from the data found in the tables compiled by *Accountancy International,* Vol. 124, August 1999, p. 8 and October 1999, p. 8.

18. See *Accountancy International,* Vol. 125, April 2000, p. 12.

19. See, for example, Aharoni (1993).

20. See Mann, Brokenbaugh, and Bargas (1999). These export and import flows include intrafirm transactions that crossed borders. The "management, consulting, and public relations services" category includes companies that are not accounting firms. It is also worth noting that for "accounting, auditing, and bookkeeping services" alone, the United States had a small net export surplus in 1998 of $15 million; larger net export surpluses were recorded in the early 1990s.

21. See Mann, Brokenbaugh, and Bargas (1999); comparable figures are not available for later years.

22. Summaries and reviews of these requirements can be found in OECD (1996, 1997) and WTO (1998). Management consulting is generally not considered to be a profession in the same sense as accounting (or law or medicine) and is generally less regulated, but some of the restrictions discussed later in this chapter (for example, restrictions on the mobility of personnel, restrictions on payments, inadequate protection for intellectual property, and "buy national" policies by governments) apply to management consulting as well.

23. For a summary of the variations in accounting regulations across the United States, see AICPA/NASBA (1998).

24. See, for example, OECD (1996, 1997), IFAC (1995), USITC (1996a, 1996b, 1997, 1998), Hegarty (1997), and WTO (1998).

25. See Macrae (1981) and Rossi (1986).

26. See, for example, OECD (1996, 1997), IFAC (1995), USITC (1996a, 1996b, 1997, 1998), Hegarty (1997), and WTO (1998).

27. See, for example, Ascher (1999).

28. Harmonization of accounting standards has received extensive discussion in the academic accounting literature; see, for example, Nobes (1996), Wyatt (1997), and Mueller (1997).
29. See the discussion of harmonization in White (1996).
30. See White (1996).
31. For discussions of these differential adaptations, see Pownall and Schipper (1999) and Gebhardt (2000).
32. For a recent commentary, see McGregor (1999).
33. The SEC has, however, since 1990 (through its Rule 144A) permitted private offerings to institutional and sophisticated investors of the securities of non-U.S. companies without requiring restatements to U.S. GAAP.
34. See Bloomer (1999).
35. See, for example, Sutton (1997).
36. A comparison between the listing of the barriers to trade in accounting services in chapter 5 and the listing of the major liberalizing provisions of the GATS in this chapter yields an apparent disconnect. The reasons for the discrepancy are threefold: first, not all countries are members of the GATS; second, as is discussed in the text below, not all members of the GATS have scheduled the accountancy sector for liberalization commitments; and third, the provisions of the GATS will not come into force until the conclusion of the round of negotiations that began in 2000.
37. See also, for example, Altinger and Enders (1996) for a more extended discussion of the GATS provisions.
38. In the descriptions that immediately follow, liberal use of the exact language of the GATS will be made.
39. However, countries can specifically exempt a sector from MFN treatment.
40. It is important to note that even when a member country decides to commit (bind) itself with respect to a specific services sector, it can nevertheless do so with restrictions that limit the application of the GATS provisions discussed below. A member can list restrictions for an individual country, or it can "horizontally" list restrictions that apply across a number of sectors.
41. The disciplines specifically state that they are not meant to apply to measures that are covered under the commitment (scheduling) provisions of Articles XVI and XVII. This absence of application was among the reasons for the IFAC's tepid endorsement of the disciplines. For a more extensive discussion of the disciplines and the negotiation process, see Ascher (1999).

42. As Ascher (1999) notes, the WPPS concluded that the harmonization of accounting frameworks was not a major goal for the disciplines, since the frameworks were primarily within the purview of the IOSCO and the IASC.
43. For a similar conclusion, see Altinger and Enders (1996).
44. Constituent countries of the European Union are counted separately.
45. In addition to the EU, the developed countries included the United States, Japan, Canada, Australia, New Zealand, Norway, and Switzerland.
46. See WTO (1998, 1999). Among the major developing countries that are members of the WTO but that did *not* make specific commitments with respect to accountancy were Egypt, India, Indonesia, Pakistan, and the Philippines.
47. See Ascher (1999).
48. See USITC (1996a, 1996b, 1997, 1998) and WTO (1998, 1999); see also Altinger and Enders (1996).
49. This pattern is consistent with the pattern of commitments across all services in general; see Altinger and Enders (1996).
50. Despite the presence of the guidelines on MRAs, progress toward achieving actual MRAs has been slow (WTO 1998). This is not surprising, since the process of determining the equivalency of qualifications—for the purpose of consumer protection—is difficult indeed. Though this problem may not be quite so apparent for accounting, it is starkly apparent for physicians. Also, it is worth noting that even within the United States, the fifty states (which are the local regulators of the accountancy profession) have had difficulties in achieving MRAs among themselves.
51. This statement does not mean that the large international accounting firms are wholly free of the potential conflicts of interest that are always present when a company audit may reveal information that may displease incumbent management—the party that has hired the auditor and that usually has the power to reengage the auditor for the following year. The potential conflicts are even more serious when a "sister" management consulting arm of the auditing firm may also be engaged by the audited company. But the greater reputations of the large firms mean that they have more to lose from subsequent revelations of shoddy work, which in turn should make them less likely to be tempted to stray.
52. See WTO (1998) and Muis (1999).
53. See, for example, McKee and Garner (1992, 1996), Riahi-Belkaoui (1994), Saudagaran and Diga (1997), and McKee, Garner, and McKee (1998).

References

Aharoni, Yair. 1993. "Ownerships, Networks, and Coalitions." In *Coalitions and Competition: The Globalization of Professional Business Services,* ed. Yair Aharoni. New York: Routledge, 121–42.

Altinger, Laura, and Alice Enders. 1996. "The Scope and Depth of GATS Commitments." *The World Economy* 19 (May): 307–32.

American Institute of Certified Public Accountants (AICPA) and National Association of State Boards of Accountancy (NASBA). 1998. *Digest of State Accountancy Laws and State Board Regulations.* New York: AICPA and NASBA.

Ascher, Bernard. 1999. "Trade Disciplines for Regulation: Lessons from the Accountancy Sector." Paper delivered at the Conference on (R)Evolution of Quality and Competency Assurance in the Global Marketplace, June 2–4, Santa Fe, N.Mex.

Bloomer, Carrie, ed. 1999. *The IASC-U.S. Comparison Project: A Report on the Similarities and Differences between IASC Standards and U.S. GAAP.* 2d ed. Norwalk, Conn.: Financial Accounting Standards Board.

Doogar, Rajib, and Robert F. Easley. 1998. "Concentration without Differentiation: A New Look at the Determination of Audit Market Concentration." *Journal of Accounting and Economics* 25 (June): 217–53.

Fox, Nancy Ruth, and Lawrence J. White. 1997. "U.S. Ocean Shipping Policy: Going against the Tide." *Annals of the American Academy of Political and Social Science* 553 (September): 75–86.

Gebhardt, Gunther. 2000. "The Evolution of Global Standards of Accounting." In *Brookings-Wharton Papers on Financial Services 2000,* ed. Robert E. Litan and Anthony M. Santomero. Washington, D.C.: Brookings Institution.

Goldberg, Lawrence G., and Lawrence J. White. 2001. "The Role of Banks in Transition Economies." In *Economies in Transition: Conception, Status, and Prospects,* ed. Peter Koveos, Yvonne Teodorovic, and Alan Young. River Edge, N.J.: World Scientific Publishing Co.

Hegarty, John. 1997. "Accounting for the Global Economy: Is National Regulation Doomed to Disappear?" *Accounting Horizons* 11 (December): 75–90.

International Federation of Accountants (IFAC). 1995. *IFAC Questionnaire on Issues Related to International Trade in Accountancy Services: Summary of Responses.* New York: IFAC, July 1.

———. 1998. "IFAC Welcomes WTO's Rules for the Accountancy Sector—But Urges Further Progress." Press release, December 17.

Macrae, Edwin W. 1981. "Impediments to a Free International Market in Accounting and the Effects on International Accounting Firms." In *The International World of Accounting: Challenges and Opportunities,* ed. John C. Burton. Reston, Va.: Council of Arthur Young Professors, 143–53.

Mann, Michael A., Laura L. Brokenbaugh, and Sylvia Bargas. 1999. "U.S. International Services: Cross-Border Trade in 1998 and Sales through Affiliates in 1997." *Survey of Current Business* 79 (October): 48–95.

McGregor, Warren. 1999. "An Insider's View of the Current State and Future Direction of International Accounting Standard Setting." *Accounting Horizons* 13 (June): 159–68.

McKee, David L., and Don E. Garner. 1992. *Accounting Services, the International Economy, and Third World Development.* Westport, Conn.: Praeger.

———. 1996. *Accounting Services, Growth, and Change in the Pacific Basin.* Westport, Conn.: Quorum.

McKee, David L., Don E. Garner, and Yosra AbuAmara McKee. 1998. *Accounting Services and Growth in Small Economies: Evidence from the Caribbean Basin.* Westport, Conn.: Quorum.

Mills, Patti A., and Joni J. Young. 1999. "From Contract to Speech: The Courts and CPA Licensing Laws, 1921–1996." *Accounting, Organizations, and Society* 24 (April): 243–62.

Most, Kenneth S. 1993. *The Future of the Accounting Profession: A Global Perspective.* Westport, Conn.: Quorum.

Mueller, Gerhard G. 1997. "Harmonization Efforts in the European Union." In *International Accounting and Finance Handbook,* ed. Frederick D. S. Choi. 2d ed. New York: John Wiley & Sons, 11-1–11-34.

Muis, Jules W. 1999. "Global Accounting, Auditing and a Financial Architecture." Prepared remarks at the SEC International Institute for Securities Market Development, April 12, Washington, D.C.

Nobes, Christopher W., ed. 1996. *International Harmonization of Accounting.* Brookfield, Vt.: Elgar.

Organization for Economic Cooperation and Development (OECD). 1996. *International Trade in Professional Services: Assessing Barriers and Encouraging Reform.* Paris: OECD.

————. 1997. *International Trade in Professional Services: Advancing Liberalization Through Regulatory Reform.* Paris: OECD.

Peltzman, Sam. 1976. "Toward a More General Theory of Regulation." *Journal of Law and Economics* 19 (August): 211–40.

Posner, Richard A. 1974. "Theories of Economic Regulation." *Bell Journal of Economics and Management Science* 5 (autumn): 335–58.

Pownall, Grace, and Katherine Schipper. 1999. "Implications of Accounting Research for the SEC's Consideration of International Accounting Standards for U.S. Securities Offerings." *Accounting Horizons* 13 (September): 259–80.

Riahi-Belkaoui, Ahmed. 1994. *Accounting in the Developing Countries.* Westport, Conn.: Quorum.

Rossi, F. A. 1986. "Government Impediments and Professional Constraints on the Operations of International Accounting Organizations." *University of Chicago Legal Forum:* 135–68.

Saudagaran, Shahrokh M., and Joselito G. Diga. 1997. "Financial Reporting in Emerging Capital Markets: Characteristics and Policy Issues." *Accounting Horizons* 11 (June): 41–64.

Stigler, George, J. 1971. "The Theory of Regulation." *Bell Journal of Economics and Management Science* 2 (spring): 3–21.

Sutton, Michael H. 1997. "Financial Reporting in U.S. Capital Markets: International Dimensions." *Accounting Horizons* 11 (June): 96–102.

U.S. International Trade Commission (USITC). 1996a. *General Agreement on Trade in Services (GATS): Examination of Major Trading Partners' Schedules of Commitments.* Publication 2940, January.

————. 1996b. *General Agreement on Trade in Services (GATS): Examination of South American Trading Partners' Schedules of Commitments.* Publication 3007, December.

————. 1997. *General Agreement on Trade in Services (GATS): Examination of Asia/Pacific Trading Partners' Schedules of Commitments* Publication 3053, August.

————. 1998. *General Agreement on Trade in Services: Examination of the Schedules of Commitments Submitted by Eastern Europe, the European Free Trade Association, and Turkey.* Publication 3127, September.

Weinstein, Grace W. 1987. *The Bottom Line: Inside Accounting Today.* New York: New American Library.

White, Lawrence J. 1988. *International Trade in Ocean Shipping Services: The United States and the World.* Cambridge, Mass.: Ballinger.

————. 1996. "Competition versus Harmonization: An Overview of International Regulation of Financial Services." In *International Trade in Financial Services,* ed. Claude Barfield. Washington, D.C.: American Enterprise Institute, 5–48.

————. 1998. "Financial Services in the United States: The Next Decade." *Business Economics* 33 (October): 27–33.

World Trade Organization (WTO), Council for Trade in Services. 1998. "Accountancy Services." Geneva: World Trade Organization, December 4.

————. 1999. "Structure of Commitments for Modes 1, 2, and 3." Geneva: World Trade Organization, March 3.

Wyatt, Arthur R. 1997. "International Accounting Standards and Organizations: Quo Vadis?" In *International Accounting and Finance Handbook,* ed. Frederick D. S. Choi. 2d ed. New York: John Wiley & Sons, 10-1–10-22.

Yarbrough, Beth V., and Robert M. Yarbrough. 1997. *The World Economy: Trade and Finance.* 4th ed. New York: Dryden Press.

Glossary of Trade Terms[*]

BINDING. A provision in a trade agreement that no tariff rate higher than the rate specified in the agreement will be imposed during the life of the agreement. Article 11 of the General Agreement on Tariffs and Trade (GATT) provides that signatories may "bind" tariff rates by including them in schedules appended to the GATT. *See* TARIFF BINDINGS.

BOUND RATES. Tariff rates resulting from GATT negotiations that are incorporated in a country's schedule of concessions and are thus enforceable as an integral element of GATT. If a CONTRACTING PARTY raises a tariff to a higher level than its bound rate, the major beneficiaries of the earlier binding have a right under the GATT to receive compensation, usually in the form of reduced tariffs on other products they export to the country. If the beneficiaries do not receive such compensation they may retaliate by raising their own tariffs against an equivalent value of the original country's exports.

CONCESSION. A tariff reduction, TARIFF BINDING, or other agreement to reduce import restrictions; usually accorded pursuant to negotiation in return for concessions by other parties.

---

*Prepared by AEI Press.

CONTESTABILITY (OF MARKETS). The actual ability of foreign firms to compete meaningfully in the market of a World Trade Organization member state, in the face of either overt legal obstruction or covert NON-TARIFF BARRIERS.

CONTRACTING PARTY. The signatory countries to the GATT. These countries have accepted the obligations and privileges of the GATT agreement.

DEBT. Securities such as bonds, notes, mortgages, and other forms of paper that indicate the intent to repay an amount owed.

DISPUTE SETTLEMENT. The resolution of opposing aims, often facilitated through an intermediary. In the GATT context, dispute settlement provides opportunities for individual contracting parties to resolve trade problems through negotiated means or with the help of a GATT panel of experts that rules on GATT legal practices and recommends solutions.

MFN TREATMENT. When one country accords another most-favored-nation (MFN) status, it agrees to extend to that country the lowest tariff rates and the same trade concessions it grants to any other MFN recipients. When a country agrees to cut tariffs on a particular product imported from one country, the tariff reduction automatically applies to imports of this product from any other country eligible for MFN treatment. The United States now applies this provision to its trade with all of its trading partners except those specifically excluded by law. All CONTRACTING PARTIES to GATT apply MFN treatment to one another under Article I of GATT, but the principle appeared in numerous bilateral trade agreements prior to the establishment of GATT. Preferential treatment accorded to developing countries, customs unions, and free trade areas all represent allowable exceptions to the MFN concept.

MUTUAL RECOGNITION AGREEMENTS (MRAS). Agreements negotiated on a sectoral basis (such as telecommunications, medical devices, pharmaceuticals, chemicals, processed foods) that allow countries to accept each other's final test results, although quality assurances may be required. Under MRAs, the entire testing and certification process may occur outside the importing country. Under MRAs with the European Community, a U.S. firm would obtain product certification on an E.C.-wide basis, enabling the firm to market its products throughout the Community. Based on private-law contractual negotiations, subcontracting permits a notified body of the European Community to delegate some of its testing responsibilities to a third-country testing lab or quality assessment body, but the notified body retains ultimate responsibility for final decisions relating to E.C. certification. Formal discussions between representatives of the U.S. Government and the European Economic Community on entering MRAs began in October 1992.

NATIONAL TREATMENT. A basic principle of international trade rules and policy. National treatment obligations generally prohibit discrimination on the basis of foreign nationality. GATT Article III, the central national treatment obligation in GATT, prohibits discrimination between imported and domestically produced goods with respect to internal taxation or other government regulation.

NON-TARIFF BARRIERS (NTBS). Any restriction or quota, charge, or policy, other than traditional customs duties, domestic support programs, discriminatory labeling and health standards, and exclusive business practices that limits the access of imported goods. NTBs may result from government or private sector actions. Such barriers have become more prevalent since the end of World War II. Since that time, tariff rates have declined significantly while other forms of protection, such as licensing and quotas, have risen. *See* Non-Tariff Measures.

Non-Tariff Measures (NTMs). These differ from NTBs only in that they are actions by governments that may have a potential for restricting international trade even though they may not always do so, such as import monitoring systems and variable levies, as well as measures that are internationally perceived as trade restrictive, even though a trade-restricting intent or effect cannot objectively be ascribed to them. Some of the most commonly used NTMs include import quotas or other quantitative restrictions, non-automatic import licensing, customs surcharges or other fees and charges, customs procedures, export subsidies, unreasonable standards or standards-setting procedures, government procurement restrictions, inadequate intellectual property protection, and investment restrictions. Participants in the Tokyo Round attempted to address these barriers through the negotiations of a number of GATT codes, open for signature to all GATT members. Seven codes were negotiated during the Tokyo Round, covering customs valuations, import licensing, subsidies and countervailing duty, antidumping duties, standards, government procurement, and trade in civil aircraft. Although the Tokyo Round codes had alleviated some of the problems caused by non-tariff measures, overall use of NTMs has increased since conclusion of the Tokyo Round. *See* Non-Tariff Barriers.

Offer list. A selected list of measures through which a country participating in trade negotiations proposes to broaden access to its market in exchange for comparable concessions from its trading partners. A country's initial offer list during a given "round" of negotiations represents its early response to the REQUEST LISTS submitted by its trading partners and may subsequently be lengthened or shortened, depending upon the responses of other countries to its own REQUEST LISTS. In addition to proposals for broadening market access through tariff reductions and expanded coverage under codes of conduct, offer lists may suggest exceptions to an agreed formula for tariff reductions on all other products. *See* REQUEST LIST.

PANEL OF EXPERTS. An ad hoc group of experienced individuals with specialized skills established for specified purposes. Under GATT dispute settlement procedures, for example, panels composed of three to five trade policy experts may be designated to arbitrate disagreements over trade policy between governments with differing interpretations of their GATT obligations.

POSITIVE/NEGATIVE LIST. A term used in the GATS negotiations. Under rules providing for a negative list, a World Trade Organization member lists only those sectors and subsectors that it will *not* agree to liberalize; all others become subject to whatever trade liberalization rules have been negotiated. Under rules providing for a positive list, a WTO member only commits to liberalize those sectors listed in the offering; all others are not subject to liberalized rules.

REQUEST/OFFER. A negotiating approach whereby requests are submitted by a country to a trading partner identifying the CONCESSIONS another seeks through negotiations. Compensating offers are similarly tabled and negotiated by delegates of the countries involved.

REQUEST LIST. A list submitted by a country to a trading partner at an early stage of trade negotiations identifying the

CONCESSIONS it seeks through the negotiations. *See* OFFER LIST.

RETALIATION. Action taken by a country to restrain its imports from another country that has violated a trade agreement or imposed other unfair trade barriers or measures that adversely affect the first country's exports. The GATT permits an adversely affected CONTRACTING PARTY to impose limited restraints on imports from another CONTRACTING PARTY that has raised its trade barriers (after consultations with countries whose trade might be affected). In theory, the volume of trade affected by such retaliatory measures should approximate the value of trade affected by the precipitating change in import protection.

RETROCESSION. The withdrawal of a pending liberalization offer.

ROLLBACK. An agreement among Uruguay Round participants to dismantle all trade-restrictive or distorting measures that are inconsistent with the provisions of the GATT. Measures subject to rollback would be phased out or brought into conformity within an agreed time frame, no later than by the formal completion of the negotiations. The rollback agreement is accompanied by a commitment to a "standstill" on existing trade-restrictive measures. Rollback is also used to refer to the imposition of quantitative restrictions at levels less than those occurring in the present. *See* STANDSTILL.

STANDSTILL. A commitment of GATT CONTRACTING PARTIES not to impose new trade-restrictive measures during the Uruguay Round negotiations.

TARIFF BINDINGS. The agreement by CONTRACTING PARTIES to maintain the duty rates on specified goods at negotiated levels or below. Bindings are provided for in GATT Article II. *See* BINDING.

TARIFF SCHEDULES OF THE UNITED STATES ANNOTATED. Effective 1979 to January 1989, the U.S. import statistics were initially collected and compiled in terms of the commodity classifications in the Tariff Schedules of the United States Annotated, an official publication of the U.S. International Trade Commission embracing the legal text of the Tariff Schedules of the United States (TSUS), together with statistical annotations. This publication was superseded by the Harmonized Tariff Schedule of the United States Annotated for Statistical Reporting Purposes in January 1989. Effective 1979 to January 1989, the U.S. export statistics were initially collected and compiled in terms of the commodity classifications in Schedule B, Statistical Classification of Domestic and Foreign Commodities Exported from the United States. Schedule B is a U.S. Bureau of the Census publication and, during this period, was based on the framework of the TSUS. In January 1989, this publication was replaced by Schedule B based on the harmonized system.

TRANSPARENCY. The extent to which laws, regulations, agreements, and practices are open, clear, measurable, and verifiable. Some of the codes of conduct negotiated during the Tokyo Round sought to increase the transparency of NON-TARIFF BARRIERS that impede trade. *See* NON-TARIFF BARRIERS.

WORKING PARTY. A specialized intergovernmental body established by a higher body to study a particular set of issues and report its findings, and often recommendations, to the higher body. In GATT, for example, a working party may be designated by the CONTRACTING PARTIES to consider a specialized trade policy problem, such as the formation of a customs union. Its recommendations may include suggestions regarding actions that specific CONTRACTING PARTIES might take. Such working parties are customarily open to all countries that wish to participate.

About the Author

Lawrence J. White is the Arthur E. Imperatore Professor of Economics at New York University's Stern School of Business and an adjunct scholar of the American Enterprise Institute. He has served as a senior staff economist at the Council of Economic Advisers, as director of the Economic Policy Office in the Antitrust Division of the U.S. Department of Justice, and as a member of the Federal Home Loan Bank Board. He is the author of many books, including *The S&L Debacle: Public Policy Lessons for Bank and Thrift Regulation* (Oxford University Press, 1991) and *U.S. Public Policy toward Network Industries* (AEI-Brookings Joint Center for Regulatory Studies, 1999), and was the North American editor of the *Journal of Industrial Economics,* 1984–1987 and 1990–1995.